WORLD OF KNOWLEDGE
ECOLOGY

BELITHA PRESS

This edition published in 2002 by
Belitha Press
A member of Chrysalis Books plc
64 Brewery Road, London N7 9NT

Typeset by Chambers Wallace, London
Printed in China
British Library Cataloguing in Publication Data
for this book is available from the British Library.

ISBN 184138 463 1

Acknowledgements

Photographic credits:

Aspect Picture Library 23
Susan Griggs/McIntyre 51 top
Susan Griggs/Howarth 51 bottom
Robert Harding Picture Library 21 top
John Hillelson 14 bottom, 21 bottom, 28
Jimmy Holmes 49
Magnum 5, 11 top, 25, 38
Massey Ferguson 17 top
D. C. Money 32, 50
Marion and Tony Morrison 9 top, 14 top, 16 bottom,
    45
Natural Science Photos 11 middle & bottom, 12
    bottom, 37, 39, 48, 58, 59
Oxford Scientific Films 12 top, 35, 36, 43, 53
Panos Pictures 27, 42
Planet Earth 57
Frank Spooner 17 bottom, 30, 31
Telegraph Colour Library 4
Thames Water Authority 33

Illustrated by: David Holmes and Eugene Fleury

This book is based on an original text by: Stephen
Seidenberg

Series editor: Neil Champion
Text adaptation: Janine Amos
Educational consultant: Carolyn Kain
Editorial: Dee Turner and Kate Scarborough
Designed by: Groom and Pickerill
Picture research and art editing: Ann Usborne

Contents

Words found in **bold** are explained
in the glossary on pages 60 and 61

Only One Earth

▲ Some plants and animals need only water for life. But others need air and land as well.

▶ Our Earth is a watery planet. This makes it possible for life to exist on the Earth.

CHAPTER ONE

LIFE ON EARTH

Earth is the only one of the nine planets in our **solar system** where plants and animals live. Living things need air, water and a temperature that is not too hot or too cold. Earth has all of these. However, there are some places, such as hot deserts and frozen wastes, where little can survive.

The environment
The part of the Earth where a plant or animal lives is called its **environment**. This may be in the air, in the ocean or on the land.

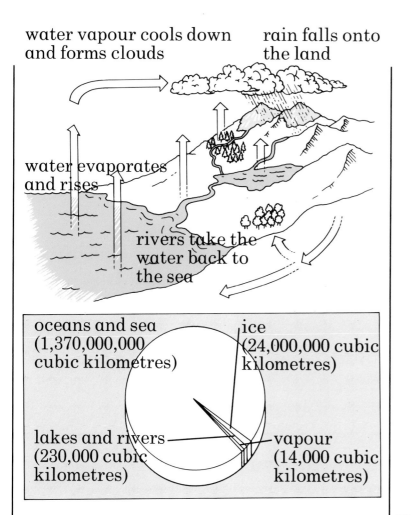

water vapour cools down and forms clouds

rain falls onto the land

water evaporates and rises

rivers take the water back to the sea

oceans and sea
(1,370,000,000 cubic kilometres)

ice
(24,000,000 cubic kilometres)

lakes and rivers
(230,000 cubic kilometres)

vapour
(14,000 cubic kilometres)

◀ The Sun heats the water in the sea and makes it evaporate – turn to vapour. The vapour rises, cools and forms clouds of water droplets. These later form larger drops, which fall as rain. Some of it falls onto the land. It then runs into rivers and flows back to the sea. This movement of water, from the sea to the sky and back again, is called the water cycle.

◀ Most of the world's water is in the oceans and seas. The rest is in rivers, lakes, ice and in the atmosphere.

Ecology is the study of living things and their environments.

Damage by people

As long as there is the right mix of air, water and heat, plants and animals can live well in their environment. But we damage the environment. We pollute the air by pumping out smoke and gases. We pollute seas and rivers by dumping rubbish, sewage and chemicals. We also damage plants and animals.

▲ A beach is damaged by oil spilled from a tanker. The oil can kill birds and fishes.

The Chain of Life

▼ Krill eat tiny plankton. Small fish eat krill, but then become food for large fish. Seals eat large fish, and people eat seals.

More than one million different kinds of plants and animals live on the Earth. Each kind, or species, is different from all the other species.

Building blocks of life

All plants and animals use the same **chemicals** as building blocks of life. These are carbon, nitrogen, oxygen and hydrogen. Plants and animals get these chemicals from their surroundings. For example, plants get their nitrogen from the soil. And we breathe in oxygen from the air.

Ocean food chain

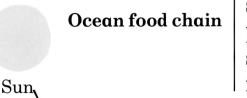

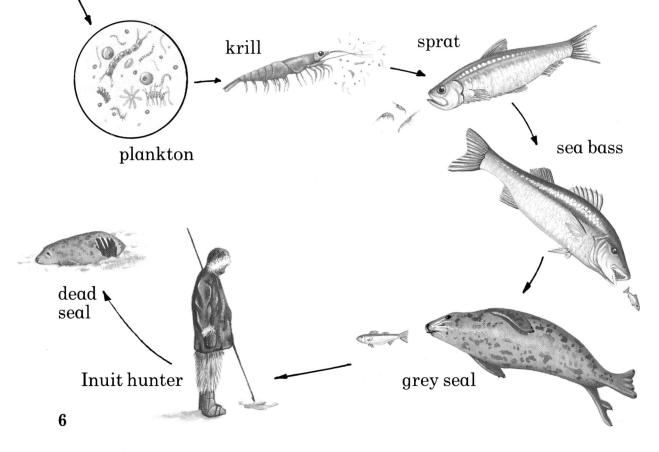

Sun

plankton

krill

sprat

sea bass

dead seal

Inuit hunter

grey seal

The food chain

Animals cannot live without plants. Green plants use energy from the Sun to help them make food. Some animals feed on the plants. Then these animals are eaten by others. The animals and plants form what scientists call a food chain. Food chains are easily broken. Farmers sometimes use chemicals to kill insects. As a result, the shrews do not have enough insects to eat. So many of the shrews die. And the owls that eat shrews go hungry. So some of the owls die too.

▼ In a forest food chain, caterpillars eat tree leaves. Small birds eat caterpillars. The hawk and other birds of prey eat the small birds. When the hawk dies, beetles and other insects feed on its body. Waste from the insects goes into the soil. The tree then feeds from these substances in the soil.

Forest food chain

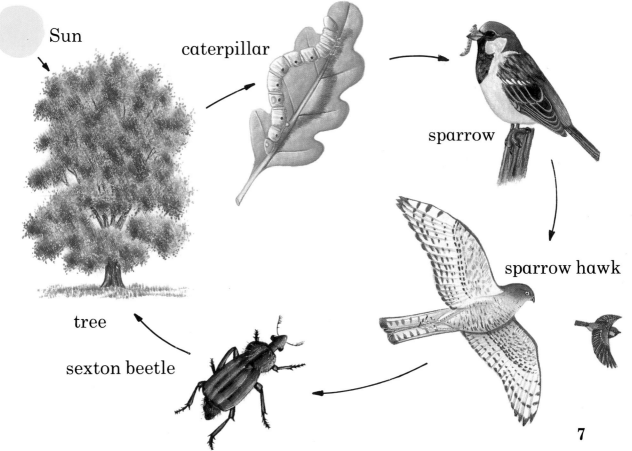

Sun

caterpillar

sparrow

sparrow hawk

tree

sexton beetle

Pollution

▼ Acid rain damages trees. They lose their leaves.

Every day we harm the environment. We dirty the air with smoke and gases. We dump rubbish and harmful chemicals into rivers, lakes and seas. And we poison the land with **fertilizers** and **pesticides**. The presence of harmful substances is called pollution.

Kinds of pollution

Most pollution is caused by industry. Power stations and cars give off poisonous gases. These

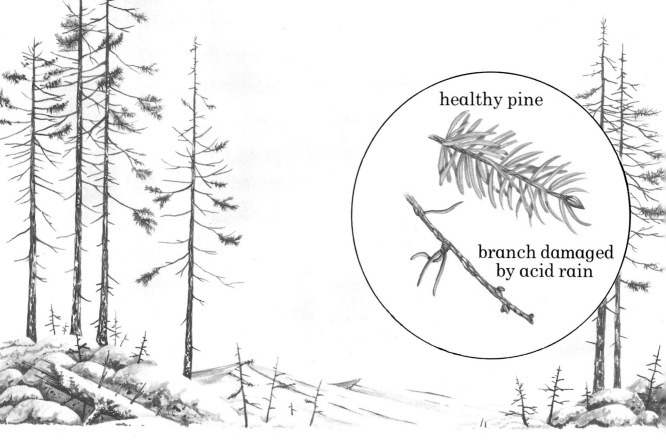

healthy pine

branch damaged by acid rain

gases can turn the rain into acid, which damages trees and crops. Factories pump out waste chemicals into rivers and streams. And we put our own rubbish and sewage into the seas and oceans. Another cause of pollution at sea is oil spilt from tankers.

Stopping pollution
It is hard to stop pollution. For we need power stations, factories and cars. But laws must be passed to stop the more dangerous forms of pollution. We must find ways to clean up the environment.

▲ A smoky fog, called smog, hangs over Mexico City. It is unhealthy to breathe smog.

▼ This beach has been polluted. The water is dirty with oil and chemicals. And rubbish is scattered on this land.

The Earth's Crust

▶ Rivers carry soil down to the sea, where it forms a layer of mud.

CHAPTER TWO
THE LAND

The centre of the Earth is very hot. This is called the core. We live on the cooler, outer layer of the Earth. This is called the crust. Most species of animals and plants live in or on the crust.

Soil

Much of the land is covered with soil. This is made up of tiny pieces or rock and dead plants and animals. These materials trap water and air. Tiny living things make the soil rich. Many plants can grow in rich soil.

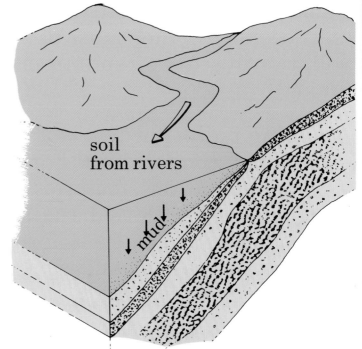

soil from rivers

mud

Making soil

Soil takes a long time to form. It is made by wind and water wearing away the rocks. It may take 1,000 years to make a layer of soil measuring no more than one centimetre deep.

Soil is lost much more quickly than it is made. Each year, 75,000 million tonnes of soil are lost. Some soil is blown away by the wind. Some is washed away by the rain. This makes it very important for us to take care of the land. For we need the soil to grow grass, forests and crops. Much erosion could be avoided if people took care of the soil.

▲ On Earth, there are cold wastelands (top), rich farmlands (middle) and wet rain forests (above).

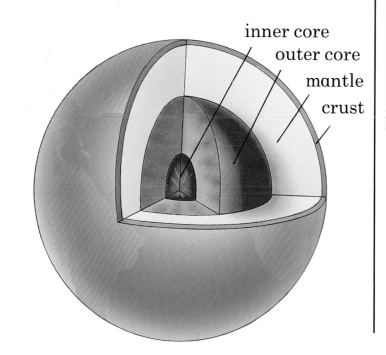

inner core
outer core
mantle
crust

◀ Compared with the inner parts of our planet, the crust is quite thin.

Life in the Soil

▶ This map shows the amount of good farm land in each region.

North America 22%

good soil

South America 19%

▲ Earthworms and wood ants eat dead plants and animals. The waste material produced helps to make the soil rich.

Healthy soil is full of life. It is home to animals such as worms and insects. Soil also contains **micro-organisms**. These are simple forms of life that are too small to see without a **microscope**. Just a spoonful of soil may hold hundreds of millions of micro-organisms.

Healthy soil
The creatures of the soil are very important for all life on Earth. For example, worms break tiny pieces of soil into smaller pieces. Worm tunnels allow air and rainwater into the soil. Some micro-

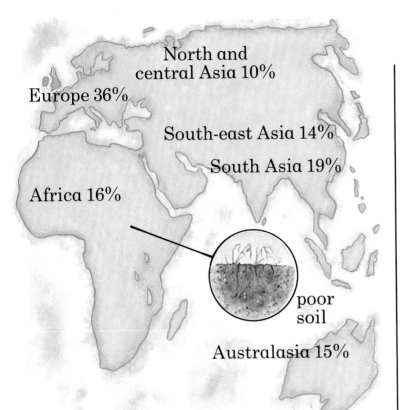

North and central Asia 10%

Europe 36%

South-east Asia 14%

South Asia 19%

Africa 16%

poor soil

Australasia 15%

organisms help trap gases in the soil. Plants use these gases to grow. So the food chain begins with micro-organisms. Other plants and animals depend on them.

Different soils

Not all soil is the same. Most soil is not good for farming. Some soil is not deep enough. Many soils don't contain enough micro-organisms or small animals. The climate is also important. If soil is too dry, cold or wet, it is not good for farming. Some countries have much more good quality farm land than others.

Earth facts

● One hectare of good soil may contain 300 million tiny creatures, such as insects, worms and millipedes.

● The rich soils in northern China and eastern USA can be as much as 150 metres thick. But Norway's thin soil averages only 10 centimetres thick.

● There are 1,500 million hectares of farmland in the world. But **erosion** ruins one million hectares every year.

● Rich soil produces four times as much food as poor soil.

● Farmers in Britain and Japan use 45 times as much fertilizer as Nigerian farmers for the same area of land. As a result, the land produces seven times as much grain as Nigerian land.

● Only about two-thirds of the world's farm land is used to grow food. The rest is used for grazing animals. In Europe, about four-fifths of farm land is used for crops. But South America, with little farm land, uses only one-fifth of it for crops.

Losing Soil

▲ Trees and small plants once grew on these hillsides. Farmers cleared them to make farm land. But rain washed the soil from the bare slopes.

We cannot live without healthy soil. Yet we destroy about 3,000 tonnes of it every second. This is a waste of a resource that we cannot replace.

Erosion

Soil is carried away naturally by water and wind. This is called **erosion**. The soil is usually carried into the oceans, where it is lost. Natural erosion usually happens very slowly. But we are speeding up erosion by clearing plants from the soil. Leaves protect the soil from the wind and rain. And roots help to bind the soil together. When the soil is left bare it is unprotected. So erosion occurs more rapidly.

► Dust storms were common in the western USA in the 1930s. Farmers had left the soil bare. So the winds blew the soil away in huge black clouds.

water erosion

wind erosion

Careless farming

Some farmers let their animals graze for too long in one place. The animals eat all the plants and leave the ground bare. Once the soil is bare, it is soon washed or blown away.

Farmers can also cause damage by over-watering the land. Too much water kills plants and harms the soil. Also, the farmers in some countries put salty water on their crops. The salt stays in the soil and may kill the plants.

▲ Wind and water are two causes of erosion. Wind can blow soil away and carve bare rock into strange shapes (top). Water can wash away soil and carve deep channels (left).

Did you know?

Erosion of the soil can occur even when crops are growing. If the crops have been sown in rows, a lot of soil is left exposed. So it is easily carried away by the wind and rain.

15

Saving the Soil

▼ Terraces protect the soil on hillsides. The rain tends to soak into the flat 'steps', instead of rushing downhill and washing the soil away.

Farmers can slow down the erosion of their land by taking care in the way they farm it. They can stop the wind and rain from carrying away too much soil.

Windbreaks and terraces
Farmers can plant trees and hedges around fields. These act as **windbreaks**. They protect the soil by slowing down the wind.

Rain-water builds up speed as it runs downhill. The faster the water flows, the more soil it carries away. But steps, called **terraces**, can be cut into the

hillsides. Doing this reduces the speed of the water. So there is less erosion of the soil.

Ways of ploughing

Farmers can also slow down erosion by ploughing across a slope, instead of up and down. This is called contour ploughing. It helps to slow the flow of water.

No-till ploughing is another way of slowing down erosion. After harvesting, farmers leave the cut stalks in the soil. New seeds are sown without turning over (tilling) the land. So the soil is never left exposed.

Did you know?

Farmers have known for a long time about building terraces to stop erosion. Some farmers have started using special ploughing techniques to reduce erosion.

◄ In no-till ploughing, the seeds are drilled into the ground. The soil is never cut up or laid bare. This protects the soil from erosion.

▼ Windbreaks like these keep soil from blowing away.

The Air

Earth facts

- Most clouds are less that 5 kilometres (3 miles) above the Earth's surface. Jet planes fly at about 10 kilometres (6 miles) up.

- When Earth was a new planet, the air had little oxygen. The gases in the atmosphere came from volcanoes. Later, green plants growing in the oceans added oxygen to the atmosphere. Plants still provide much of the oxygen we breathe.

- The further you go above sea level, the thinner the air becomes. This is why climbers on high mountains wear oxygen masks. They soon feel 'out of breath' if they breathe the thin air.

▶ Plants take in a gas called carbon dioxide from the air. They give off oxygen. Cows breathe in oxygen and make wastes after eating plants. Their dung contains nitrogen, which helps new plants grow.

CHAPTER THREE
EARTH'S ATMOSPHERE

Around the Earth is a layer of gases. We call this layer the **atmosphere**. The gases in the atmosphere make up the air that we breathe.

How the atmosphere helps us
The atmosphere helps life in other ways. In the daytime, it blocks out harmful **rays** from the Sun. At night, the atmosphere acts like a blanket, keeping the Earth warm.

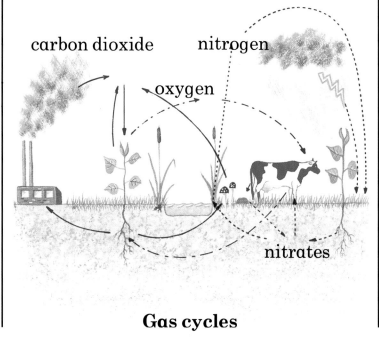

carbon dioxide   nitrogen

oxygen

nitrates

Gas cycles

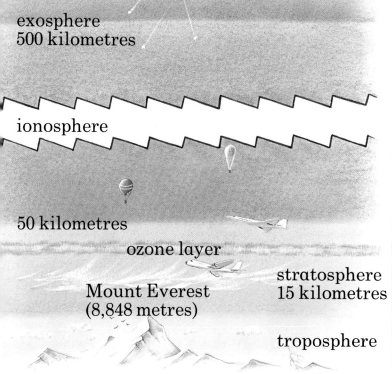

exosphere
500 kilometres

ionosphere

50 kilometres

ozone layer

Mount Everest
(8,848 metres)

stratosphere
15 kilometres

troposphere

◄ The main division of the Earth's atmosphere. Above the ionosphere is the exosphere. Here the atmosphere gradually thins out into space.

nitrogen

oxygen

argon

carbon dioxide

neon

▲ The atmosphere is made up of many gases. Nitrogen and oxygen are the most abundant.

The atmosphere also protects the Earth from lumps of rock called meteoroids. These move through space at high speed. Sometimes they approach the Earth. They get very hot when they pass through the atmosphere. Most of them burn up before they reach the ground.

Gases in the atmosphere

The atmosphere contains many gases, mainly nitrogen and oxygen. Smoke, dust, water **vapour** and micro-organisms are present too. The atmosphere is divided into layers. The layer closest to the ground is called the troposphere.

Did you know?

The environment is divided into three parts: the air (atmosphere), the land and the water. The atmosphere is larger than the other parts. Traces of gases from the Earth are found up to about 1,000 kilometres (over 600 miles) above sea level.

Air Pollution

Earth facts

● In 1952, over 4,000 people in London died from air pollution. Now new laws keep London air cleaner.

● Each year factories in Europe give off 40 million tonnes of sulphur dioxide, a polluting gas.

● Acid rain has killed almost half the fish that lived in the lakes of southern Norway.

● Over half the trees in West Germany's Black Forest have been damaged by acid rain.

▶ Factories, power stations and cars give off gases. The gases mix with water in the air to form acid clouds. These produce harmful acid rain.

Air has no colour and no smell. We can see or smell air only when it is **polluted**.

Dirty air

Dirty air can make us ill. Plants and animals are harmed by air pollution too. Buildings can crumble away if air pollution eats away the stone. And air pollution can even cause harm to the atmosphere itself.

There are two kinds of pollution. There are gases that do not belong in the atmosphere. And there are tiny bits of liquid, soot

Acid rain cycle

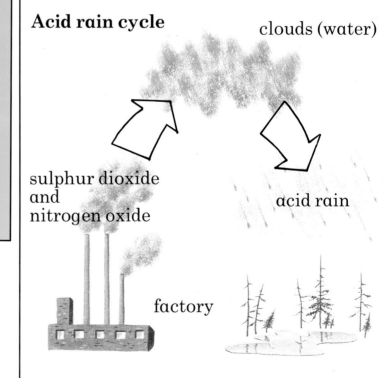

clouds (water)

sulphur dioxide and nitrogen oxide

acid rain

factory

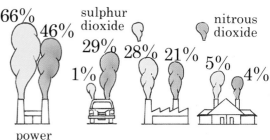

66%	46%	sulphur dioxide	29%	28%	21%	nitrous dioxide 5%	4%
power stations		1% vehicles		factories		homes	

▲ Sources of polluting gases in Britain.

◄ This temple (in Athens, Greece) has been standing for thousands of years. Now it is falling down because air pollution is eating away the stone.

▼ Air pollution is bad in Tokyo, Japan. Many people wear masks to keep the dirty air out of their lungs.

or dust. Both kinds of pollution come from burning coal, oil and gas for energy.

Fossil fuels

Coal, oil and gas are called **fossil fuels**. We burn them to run cars and factories. Fossil fuels also provide energy to make electricity and to heat our homes. Fossil fuels are useful – but they are also harmful. When fossil fuels are burnt, sulphur dioxide and nitrogen oxide gases are sent up into the air. These gases cause **acid rain**, one of the worst kinds of air pollution. It damages plants, animals and buildings.

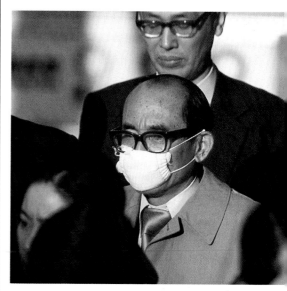

Polluted Poland

Poland is one of the most polluted countries in the world. Acid rain there has been known to eat into metal railway tracks!

Poisons in the Air

▼ Some forms of pollution put extra carbon dioxide gas into the air. This gas acts like the glass in a greenhouse. It lets the Sun's rays through, but doesn't let much heat out. This keeps the Earth warm. But too much carbon dioxide could cause over-heating and change our climate.

The gases we put into the air mix with those already in the atmosphere. Acid rain is just one deadly mixture made in this way.

The greenhouse effect

The atmosphere that surrounds the Earth acts like the glass of a greenhouse. The atmosphere lets the Sun's rays through to the Earth. They warm the Earth, and the atmosphere traps the heat. **Carbon dioxide** is the main gas that traps heat. Carbon dioxide is necessary for plant life. But, if there is too much of this gas, the Earth will become warmer. This will change the Earth's climate.

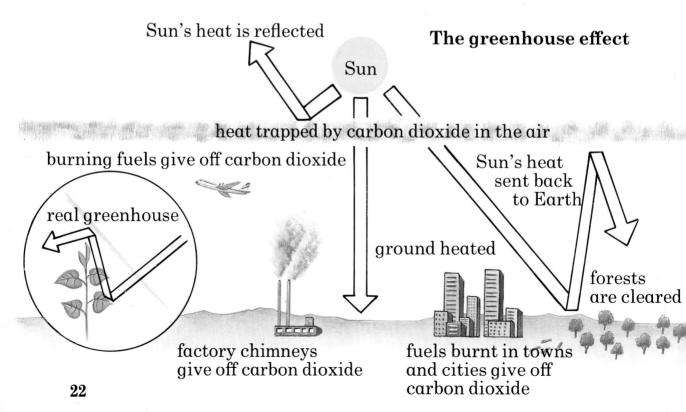

Sun's heat is reflected

Sun

The greenhouse effect

heat trapped by carbon dioxide in the air

burning fuels give off carbon dioxide

Sun's heat sent back to Earth

real greenhouse

ground heated

forests are cleared

factory chimneys give off carbon dioxide

fuels burnt in towns and cities give off carbon dioxide

◄ Los Angeles has more smog (smoky fog) than any other city in the USA.

◄ CFCs from spray cans, refrigerators and some fast food cartons can damage the ozone layer.

Ozone

Ozone is a special form of oxygen. A layer of ozone lies about 25 kilometres (16 miles) above the Earth. This layer acts as a shield. It protects the Earth against harmful rays from the Sun. But chemicals called **CFCs** damage the ozone layer. Every day we release CFCs into the Earth's atmosphere.

CFCs

Chemicals made by people can mix with the ozone layer and destroy it. These chemicals (called CFCs) keep our refrigerators cool. They are sometimes put in spray cans to force other substances out. They also make up some of the foam plastic packages used for hamburgers and other foods.

Stopping Pollution

We can reduce air pollution. Burning only high quality coal and oil can help. And **filters** can be used in power station chimneys. The filters remove the worst polluting gases from the smoke before it is released.

Engines and chemicals
Cars, buses and trucks can use **lead-free petrol** to lower the amount of lead particles that get into the air. And devices can be fitted to the exhaust pipes to trap other poisonous substances.

Some countries now limit the use of CFCs. These are the chemicals

Hydro-electric power

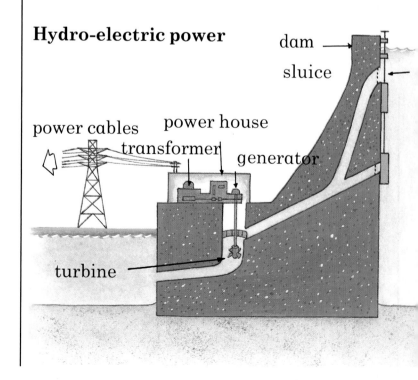

► Water power is a clean way to make electricity. Water from behind the dam is let through the sluice gate. The water turns a turbine. The turbine turns a generator, which makes electricity.

that destroy the ozone layer. The USA has banned the use of CFCs in spray cans. Britain and some other nations have cut down on the amount of CFCs they make. This helps, but we need to do more. We need to find other chemicals to take the place of the harmful CFCs.

The cure
We can all help to stop pollution. We can stop buying spray cans that use CFCs. We can tell people why they should use lead-free petrol. And we can walk or cycle more, instead of riding in cars and buses.

▲ Wind power is another clean source of energy. These machines use the power of the wind to make electricity.

Did you know?
Some people already use clean sources of energy. Wind power provides electricity in some countries. Wave power from the sea makes electricity in other parts of the world. Solar energy uses the Sun's rays to heat water in many homes.

Our Watery World

▶ Water covers more than two-thirds of the Earth's surface.

Facts and feats

● The Nile is the longest river in the world. It is 6,690 kilometres (4,160 miles) long.

● The Amazon river has the world's largest river basin. It covers an area of about 7 million square kilometres (2.7 million square miles).

● Every second, about 180,000 cubic metres of water flows from the Amazon river into the sea.

● Lake Superior in North America is the world's largest freshwater lake. It has an area of over 82,000 square kilometres (about 32,000 square miles).

● The deepest freshwater lake is Lake Baykal in the USSR. It is up to 1,940 metres deep.

CHAPTER FOUR
WATER FOR LIFE

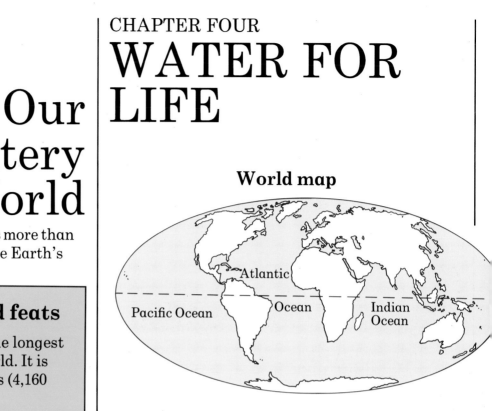

World map

Atlantic

Pacific Ocean   Ocean   Indian Ocean

From outer space the Earth looks like a blue planet. This is because the oceans cover more than two-thirds of the Earth's surface. Plants and animals can't live without water – it is necessary for all kinds of life.

The water cycle

The waters of the Earth are always moving. Water moves from the oceans, up to the air, down to the land and back to the oceans again. This is called the water cycle. The Sun's heat makes some of the water in rivers, lakes and seas rise as a gas called water vapour. Plants give off water vapour too.

The water vapour cools as it rises. This makes it change into clouds of tiny water droplets. These later join to form larger drops of rain, which fall to the ground, or into the seas.

Almost all of the Earth's water is in the seas. But sea water is salty. Most land animals and plants need fresh water to live. Of all the water on Earth, only a very small amount is fresh water.

▼ When sea water evaporates, the salt in it is left behind. These women in Sri Lanka are collecting salt from shallow pools of sea water.

Ocean Life

The oceans form the largest **zone** for life on Earth. But most of Earth's plants and animals live on land or in the air.

The oceans are very deep – 11,000 metres at the deepest point. Animals and plants live in all parts of the ocean. Some, such as jellyfish, live near the surface of the water. Others, such as most fish, live deeper in the water. Tiny plants and animals, called plankton, stay mostly below 100 metres during the day. But, at night, they come to the surface.

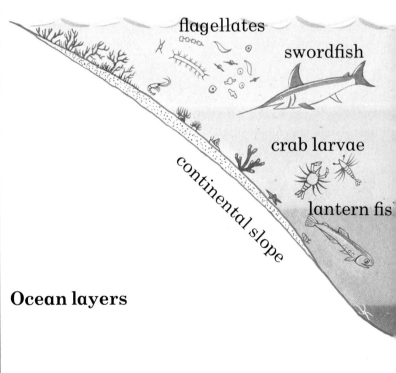

Ocean layers

flagellates

swordfish

crab larvae

continental slope

lantern fis

▲ Special submarines help scientists to study life under the sea.

The ocean depths

At the bottom of the ocean are sponges, clams and many other sea creatures. Most kinds of ocean life live deep down on the ocean floor. The sunlight cannot reach down to this depth. So it is dark, although some fish and other animals make their own light by glowing.

Of all the plants and animals on our planet, about one-fifth live in the water. Of these, nine out of every ten live on the ocean floor.

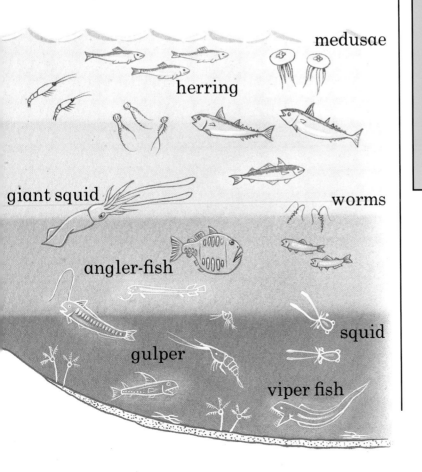

medusae

herring

giant squid

worms

angler-fish

squid

gulper

viper fish

◀ The ocean can be divided into layers. Different kinds of plants and animals live in each layer.

29

Polluting the Water

Water is important for all life on Earth. We need water to drink and to grow **crops**. We eat fish from rivers and oceans. And we get salt from the sea.

Water pollution

Even though we need water, we pollute it in many ways. We pollute rivers with our sewage. And we dump rubbish in lakes and oceans. Many factories pump dangerous chemicals into rivers and seas. Sewage and chemicals can be made safe before they are dumped. But this is expensive.

Farmers use fertilizers to help their crops grow. And they use pesticides to kill insects that damage their crops. But rain can wash these chemicals into rivers

▼ Every day this barge takes rubbish from New York City out to sea. When the barge is far from shore, it dumps the rubbish in the ocean.

and streams. In great quantities they can pollute the water. The chemicals can poison plants, fish and people.

Oil slicks

Oil pollutes water if it is spilt by accident or dumped as waste. When lots of oil enters the water, it floats on the surface. It forms a layer called a slick. Slicks spread to cover huge areas. Oil kills birds and other wildlife. A spill from one **tanker** may kill many thousands of sea birds. There are many ways of cleaning up spilt oil. But they are not much use once the oil has spread.

▲ This river looks clean but it is very polluted. A paper mill pours waste chemicals through a pipe into the water.

▲ An oil slick killed these animals.

Cleaning the Water

Water pollution harms us all. But there are many ways to keep rivers, lakes and oceans clean. Sewage can be made safe before it is drained into rivers and seas. Also, some chemicals can be treated before they are **dumped**.

Dangerous chemicals

Other chemicals need special care. Some must be burnt at high temperatures before they are safe. This is done in ships, far out to sea. Some dangerous chemicals are put in special containers before they are dumped. The containers are meant to stop the chemicals escaping.

The Mediterranean Sea

Not long ago, the Mediterranean Sea was badly polluted. Human waste was pumped into the sea.

▲ People in China grow mulberry bushes to feed silkworms. The channels supply the water that the bushes need in order to grow.

► Water from sewage goes through many stages of treatment. These make it safe to be pumped into rivers and seas.

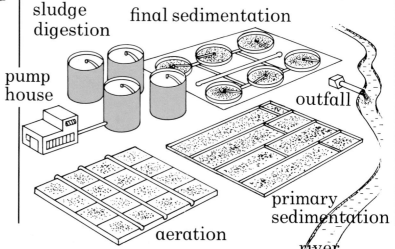

sludge digestion

final sedimentation

pump house

outfall

primary sedimentation

aeration

river

Chemicals from farms and factories polluted the sea too. Many beaches were unhealthy because there was so much pollution. In some places, it was dangerous to eat seafood, such as mussels and clams. These contained high levels of poisons. In 1976, almost all the countries surrounding the Mediterranean agreed to stop dumping wastes. Today there is less pollution, but the waters still contain some harmful chemicals.

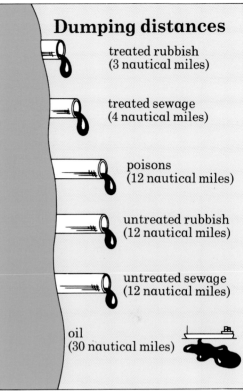

Dumping distances

treated rubbish (3 nautical miles)

treated sewage (4 nautical miles)

poisons (12 nautical miles)

untreated rubbish (12 nautical miles)

untreated sewage (12 nautical miles)

oil (30 nautical miles)

▲ This chart shows the minimum distances from shore for dumping various wastes off the coast of Britain. A nautical mile is longer than an ordinary mile. It equals 1.85 kilometres

◄ This river was once polluted. Now that it's been cleaned, fish can live in it again.

CHAPTER FIVE

Deserts

THE DRY LANDS

A true desert gets less than 25 centimetres of rain each year. Few people live in deserts because they are so dry. Deserts and the dry lands that surround them make up about one-third of the Earth's surface.

Why are there deserts?

Some lands are dry because they are far from the sea. The moist air from above the ocean falls as rain before it reaches these lands. Other deserts are in areas where dry winds blow across the land all year round.

Desert facts

● About 200 million people live in the dry lands surrounding deserts.

● The Sahara Desert, the world's largest desert, covers an area bigger than the USA.

● Some Sahara sand dunes are more than 400 metres high.

● Some deserts are sandy, some are rocky and some are made of ice.

● Nearly half the world's deserts are in cold regions. Antarctica is the largest cold desert.

● Libya recorded the highest temperature ever in 1922. The thermometer read 58°C in the shade at Al' Aziziyah in the Sahara Desert.

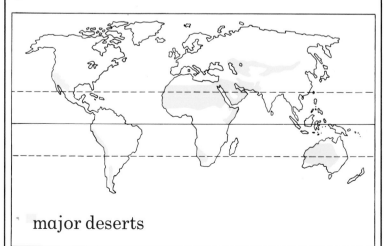

major deserts

▲ Moist air cools as it rises and forms clouds. These release this moisture as rain on the mountain. So the air that passes over the desert is dry.

▲ Rain is rare in the Kalahari Desert, in southern Africa. But, when it comes, desert plants suddenly spring up.

Other deserts have mountains nearby which block the flow of moist air. As the air tries to cross the mountains, it cools. This makes most of the moisture in the clouds fall as rain. So the land on the other side of the mountains gets very little rain. Lands in the 'shadow' of the mountains get only dry air. They are said to be in a rain-shadow.

Plant life

In hot deserts, plants grow only when the rains come. Polar deserts have plants only when the temperature rises above freezing.

tropical rain forests (10,000 mm)

temperate forests (1,000 mm)

desert (0-25 mm)

grasslands (300 mm)

▲ Yearly rainfall in various regions.

Types of Desert

▼ Only a small number of deserts have sand dunes like these. Most deserts are covered with rocky soil.

All deserts are dry for most of the time. So they have few plants and animals.

Cold deserts

Cold deserts are covered in ice. There are two kinds of cold desert. One kind has a short summer. The temperature gets high enough to melt some of the ice. So a few plants can grow.

The second kind of cold desert has almost no plants. At the Earth's poles, the temperature is below freezing all year round. The ground and the water there is always frozen. This is called a polar desert.

Hot deserts
Tropical deserts are hot all year round. **Sub-tropical** deserts have hot summers and cold winters. The Sun's heat is very strong in summer in these desert.

With so much heat reaching the ground, deserts become very hot by day. But, at night, desert temperatures fall very low. There is no moisture in the air to keep the heat from escaping.

Plant life
Desert plants have short growing seasons. In hot deserts, plants grow only when there is rain. Cold deserts warm up above freezing for only a few weeks each year. Cold desert plants can grow only during this short time.

▲ Many deserts are stony, like this one in Namibia (South West Africa).

▼ Polar deserts have temperatures below freezing all year round.

Marginal Lands

Some land is semi-arid – partly dry. This land gets more rain than a desert, but not enough for crops to grow without extra water. Semi-arid lands are often grasslands on the edges of deserts. They are sometimes called **marginal** lands.

Grasslands

There are two main types of grasslands – savannah and steppe. Savannahs are found in tropical and sub-tropical regions. They may have wet and dry seasons, with little temperature change.

The grassy plains called steppes are in colder parts of the world. Steppes have hot summers and cold winters.

▼ The Mongols and the Khazakhs are two groups of people living on the steppes in Mongolia. They roam with their herds of cattle and other animals that feed on the grass.

Food crops

Crops can be grown on marginal lands. But they must be provided with water. The soil is not rich in these areas. And farmers can't use the same fields every year for their crops. The goodness in the soil would be quickly used up. If the same land is used several years in a row, the soil becomes more like desert land.

Marginal lands are important. They provide millions of people with food supplies. But more than 200 million people are in danger of **starvation** because grasslands are being destroyed.

▲ During the wet season, the savannah in Kenya becomes very green.

Grassland to Desert

The Dust Bowl

In the early 1900s, farmers ploughed up the marginal grasslands of the Great Plains, in the USA. They planted crops, such as wheat and corn. Then dry years came in the early 1930s. Winds blew away tonnes of soil in huge clouds. The clouds blackened the sky as far as the Atlantic Ocean. An enormous area became ruined for farming. It was called the Dust Bowl. This was one of the biggest environmental disasters in the world.

The grasslands are poor farming areas. But they are good **grazing** land for sheep and goats. Travelling people called nomads move from place to place to find food and water for their herds. If the animals don't stay long in one place, the grassland is not harmed. But, if the animals eat all the grass, the bare soil is carried away by wind and rain.

Too many people

With more people in the world, farmers need to grow more food. But all the good land is already being used. So farmers are using marginal land. This means that there is less grassland for the animals. All the grass may be eaten, and the land may soon turn into desert.

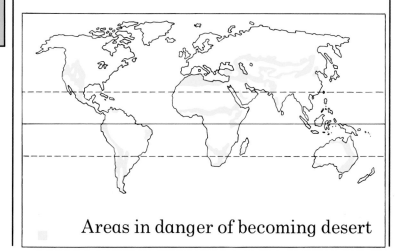

Areas in danger of becoming desert

▶ This map shows the main areas of land in danger of becoming desert.

Worn-out soil

Grassland soils are too thin for farming. Crops can grow in the soil for a few years. But then all the goodness in the soil is used up. So no more crops can be grown in that soil.

▲ Nomads live in deserts and marginal lands. They raise cattle, sheep and other animals that eat grass. Today it is hard for the nomads to find enough food and water for their animals. ▼

Desert Growth

Desert facts

● Over 60,000 square kilometres (23,000 square miles) of soil becomes desert each year. This is almost half the area of England.

● Each year, over 200,000 square kilometres (70,000 square miles) of land loses its ability to grow crops. This is more than $2\frac{1}{2}$ times the size of Scotland.

● Over one-third of the Earth's surface is desert, or is affected by desert growth.

● Africa has many deserts. Some of it has been made by people farming land that was not suitable for crops.

▶ These desert people are digging a deep well.

Deserts can grow quickly. Sometimes this is natural, but sometimes people are the cause. They may let animals eat all the grass. Or they may allow the soil to blow away when they try to farm the land. So patches of desert appear. Then the people use the good land that is left. And soon, new patches of desert appear. In time, patches link up, so that the whole area is turned into desert.

the green
'Great Wall'

older forest

Gobi Desert

new forest

CHINA

Changing farming patterns

If we are to feed everyone, we must have land to grow food on. We need grassland for our animals too. Natural weather changes can make deserts grow. We cannot stop this. But we can stop people from turning good land into desert.

Ways of farming and keeping animals can be changed. Care can be taken to stop farmers from destroying grassland in order to grow crops.

Green 'Great Wall'

◀ Long ago, forests were cleared in northern China to make way for farming. Now erosion is destroying the land. The Chinese are fighting erosion by planting a green 'Great Wall' of trees. They plan to plant bands of trees across the whole country.

Dangerous goats!

Only the right kind of animals should graze on grasslands. Goats can cause great damage to marginal land. Goats will eat almost everything that grows. They leave the soil bare and unprotected against the wind. So the grassland may be turned to desert. One way to help stop the growth of deserts is to change herding methods. Herds of goats and other animals should be reduced in size.

◀ After eating all the plants on the ground, goats may climb trees to get more food.

Where the Trees Are

▶ The rain forests grow in the tropics.

Forest facts

● The oldest living thing is a creosote plant 11,700 years old. It grows in California, USA.

● The largest living tree is 'General Sherman', a giant sequoia growing in California. It is nearly 84 metres high, and 35 metres around the base.

● The tallest tree still living is a mountain ash in Tasmania that stands 99 metres tall.

● The world's largest forest, in Siberia, covers an area of more than 10 million square kilometres (4 million square miles). This is about one-quarter of all the forest area in the world.

CHAPTER SIX

THE FORESTS

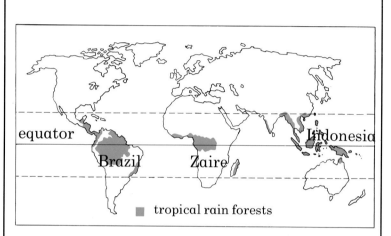

tropical rain forests

Forests are important for life on Earth. They are home to many plants and animals. We get some of our **medicines** from forest plants. Wood and paper come from forest trees. Forest plants and trees have an important effect on the weather. And forests help to make the air we breathe.

Forests make oxygen

We need forests to make oxygen, an important part of the air we breathe. Plants and trees take in carbon dioxide. They give off oxygen, which goes into the Earth's atmosphere.

Water from plants

Trees and other plants take up water from the ground through their roots. This water brings goodness from the soil.

Later, the plants release this water. The water is in the form of vapour. It is sent into the air through the leaves. This process is called **transpiration**. The water sent into the air forms clouds. This water can then fall back to the Earth again as rain.

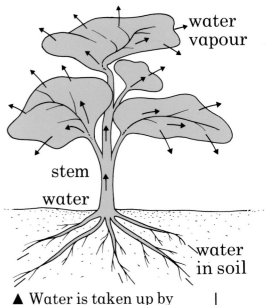

▲ Water is taken up by the roots of the plant. The water passes up the stem. The leaves release the water into the air as vapour.

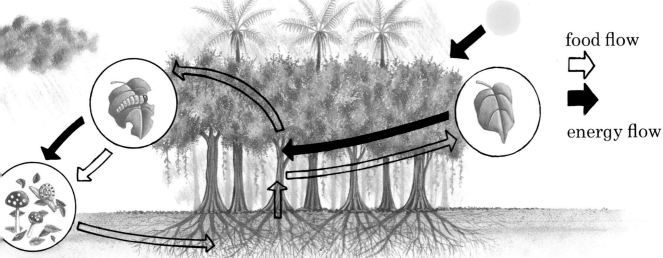

▲ The Sun helps leaves to make food for trees. Animals on the forest floor and dead leaves make the soil rich.

◄ Clouds over the forests of Peru are part of the water cycle.

45

Kinds of Forest

Forest facts

● Tropical rain forests cover only about one-tenth of the land on Earth. But they contain about half of all species of plants and animals.

● Over half the world's total rain forest area lies in three countries – Zaire, Brazil and Indonesia.

● It rains heavily in rain forests. A rain forest in Ghana may get more rain in 15 minutes than London gets in an average month.

● More kinds of trees grow around one volcano in the Philippine rain forest than there are native trees in North America.

● Bamboos are woody grasses common in rain forests. They can grow up to 60 centimetres in a day!

There are three main types of forest. Each kind is home to different plants and animals.

Tropical rain forests

Tropical rain forests grow where it is hot all year round and a lot of rain falls. Thousands of kinds of trees may grow in a rain forest. The trees have broad, flat leaves that stay green all year. About half of all the world's forests are tropical rain forests.

Temperate forests

Temperate forests grow in areas with cooler temperatures and less rainfall. In winter, the trees lose their leaves. Huge temperate forests once covered most of Europe and the eastern part of North America.

squirrel monkey

jaguar

coniferous trees   temperate forest trees

rain forest trees

Coniferous forests

Coniferous forests are made up of trees that bear **cones**. Such trees grow where the winters are long and cold and the summers are short. Coniferous leaves are needle-shaped and evergreen.

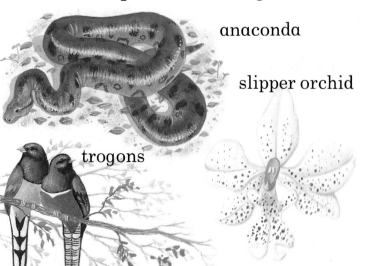

anaconda

slipper orchid

trogons

▼ There are many more species (kinds) of living things in a tropical rain forest than in the same area of temperate forest.

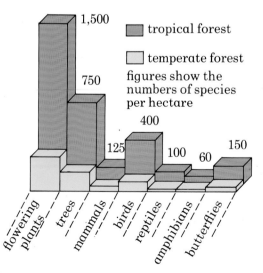

1,500

750

400

125   100   150
              60

tropical forest

temperate forest

figures show the numbers of species per hectare

flowering plants   trees   mammals   birds   reptiles   amphibians   butterflies

◄ Some plants and animals of the South American rain forest.

47

Losing Forests

All over the world, forests have disappeared. Thick forests once covered Europe and the Middle East. But people have cut down many of the trees. So there are now very few forests left. North America once had some of the largest forests the world has ever seen. By 1860, most of the forests in the United States had been destroyed.

During the last 90 years, people have cut down almost half the world's rain forests. Today, an area of forest the size of two football pitches is cut down every second! Or, to put it another way,

▲ Bulldozers cut roads into the thickest rain forests. Once there are roads, farmers use the land to grow crops or raise animals.

▶ In Morocco, farmers are cutting down forests to make more fields for crops.

a forest the size of Wales is destroyed every month.

Demand for wood

We cut down trees for many reasons. We use the wood for fuel and for making things. Farmers clear away forests so that they can grow crops or graze animals on the land. And we also clear land to build cities and roads.

Destruction

Without tree roots to hold it together, the soil is more easily washed away by rain. And the animals and plants of the forest die out.

▲ People use wood for many things, such as houses, furniture and boats. Many people have to burn wood for cooking and heating.

▲ Baskets of firewood for sale in Nepal. People in Nepal use wood for fuel, so their forests are quickly disappearing.

Saving the Trees

▲ The papaw grows in South American rain forests. The fruit is good to eat. Like other useful plants, it will disappear if the rain forests are destroyed.

▶ Rain forest soil is very thin. Most of the goodness in it comes from the layer of rotting leaves on top of the soil.

The first forests to be destroyed were in Europe and North America. In these areas, we have learnt our lesson. Forests here are now protected, and some new ones have been planted.

Rain forests in danger

Today rain forests are in danger. Once a rain forest is cut down, its environment is destroyed forever. Many plants grow in a rain forest. Most of the goodness the plants need comes from the forest floor. Here there is a layer of rotting plants and leaves. The warm weather speeds up the rotting process. So the dead plant material soon becomes food for living plants. In this way, the

rotting leaves

poor soil

rock

◀ The trees in this rain forest in Brazil were cut down for wood. But tiny seedlings are being planted to start a new forest.

goodness in plants is used again and again.

Cutting down the trees destroys this process. Without the rotting leaves, the soil is too poor to grow plants. And, without plants to protect it, wind and water soon carry the soil away. So what was once a rain forest soon turns into desert.

Hugging trees

In northern India, some people are trying to save their forests. When workers arrive with axes and saws, the people hug the trees. They hope to stop the workers from cutting down the trees.

▼ This land was once clear of trees. Now new forests have been planted.

CHAPTER SEVEN

PLANTS AND ANIMALS

So Many Kinds

guenon monkeys

▲ These guenon monkeys live only on the island of Madagascar.

▼ A drug made from the rosy periwinkle can cure some kinds of cancer.

No one knows how many different kinds of plants and animals there are on Earth. Scientists have named about $1\frac{1}{2}$ million so far. Many more are still to be discovered. Scientists keep finding more species of plants and insects living in the rain forests.

Useful plants
Plants are very important. Many of our medicines come from

plants. The rosy periwinkle, for example, grows in the Amazon rain forest. A drug produced from it has been found to cure some kinds of **cancer**.

Plants can help in other ways too. Another Amazon plant makes a liquid called **methanol**. One day methanol may be used in place of petrol in car engines. Other forest plants could be of use to us. But many are destroyed as the trees are cut down. So we are losing valuable resources every day.

Some desert plants are useful too. For example, the jojoba plant produces a very fine oil. This is now being used in industry instead of whale oil.

▼ The jojoba plant grows in North American deserts. The berries produce a fine oil that is used in industry.

Wildlife in Danger

Many kinds of plants and animals have disappeared from the Earth. They have died out and become **extinct**. This still occurs today.

Extinction

People often cause animals and plants to become extinct. We may destroy an animal's home by building or farming. We may kill off animals by hunting them. And

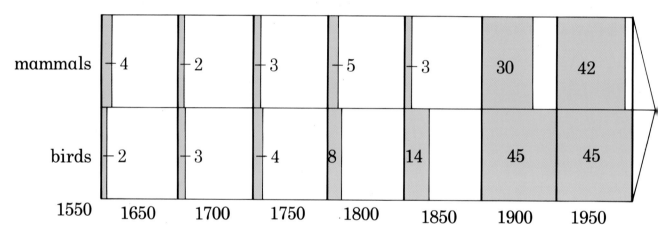

	1550	1650	1700	1750	1800	1850	1900	1950
mammals		4	2	3	5	3	30	42
birds		2	3	4	8	14	45	45

▲ This chart shows how many species of mammals and birds have become extinct in various periods since 1550.

Did you know?

Animals and plants are in danger all around the world. Asia has the biggest problem. About one-third of Asian mammal species are in danger of dying out.

wild plants may die out if too many of them are picked.

In the past, people caused the extinction of about one species of plant or animal each year. But, since 1985, we have caused almost one extinction every day. And extinction is now happening more quickly than ever before.

Long ago, most of the wildlife

passenger pigeon

killed off was on islands. When people settled on islands, they took along sheep, cattle and goats. These animals ate the grass. So there was little left for the wild animals on the islands. As a result, many island species became extinct. Also, visiting ships brought rats to the islands. The rats killed off many animals.

dodo

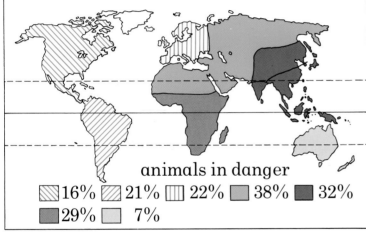

animals in danger

◫ 16% ◫ 21% ⊞ 22% ▨ 38% ■ 32%
■ 29% ▨ 7%

▲ The dodo died out in 1700, and the passenger pigeon died out in 1914. Both species were destroyed by people.

▼ Plants and animals of all kinds are under threat.

humpback whale

large blue butterfly

snake's head fritillary

panda

white rhinoceros

Californian condor

Losing Animals

▲ The North American bison, or buffalo, once lived in huge herds. But people hunted them until they almost died out.

Bamboo and the Panda

The giant panda eats only one kind of bamboo. With more land being cleared for crops, there is less land for the bamboo to grow on. If the bamboo dies out, so will the giant panda. And many other kinds of plants, insects and animals could be in danger too.

Cutting down trees and bushes and clearing grasslands can cause animals to die out. And so can hunting.

Destroying animals' homes

When people farm, build cities or make new roads, they change the environment. They may destroy an animal's home, called its habitat. Many farmers in Britain have dug up the hedges around their fields. This has taken away the homes of the birds and other animals that lived in them. Very many wildlife species can live only in one type of habitat. When that changes, they die.

Hunting

People hunt animals for food and sport. Some types of whale have been hunted for their meat until there are only a few left. The North American bison once lived in huge herds. But these were hunted for sport and were almost wiped out. Today they live on protected land.

Animals are over-hunted for other reasons too. Tigers, leopards and other big cats are threatened because their fur is used to make coats. Some snakes and crocodiles are killed to make shoes and handbags. And tortoise shells are used for jewellery.

▲ Goods are still made from the skins of rare animals. As a result, some species are in danger of extinction.

Deadly facts

● Some scientists believe that dinosaurs died out because prehistoric rats ate their eggs.

● Some scientists say that Stone Age people hunted the mastodon and the woolly mammoth until these animals died out.

● Nearly 1,000 kinds of animals and over 20,000 kinds of plants are in danger.

● In Java, all but about 50 Javanese rhinoceroses have died.

◄ Some kinds of whales are almost extinct. But people from Japan and the USSR still hunt whales.

Saving Wildlife

▶ Old Faithful Geyser in Yellowstone National Park, USA. It shoots boiling water into the air. Yellowstone was the world's first national park.

National parks

There are over 2,000 national parks and wildlife reserves in the world. Many tourists visit the national parks in Kenya and Tanzania. The visitors pay to watch and photograph the wildlife.

It is important that we stop animals and plants from dying out. Protecting wildlife is called conservation.

Protecting habitats

Most plants and animals die out because we destroy their habitats. But we can save their homes by protecting forests and other wild areas. We must make good use of the farmland we have, instead of using up marginal land.

Wildlife reserves and national parks are important habitats for wildlife. The land here cannot be cleared for farming. And hunting is against the law.

Zoos and rare-breed centres preserve animals from extinction. Zoos help the animals to breed in safety. Some of the animals may be returned to their natural homes when they are old enough.

Many countries now have laws that protect wildlife. These laws stop some species of animals and plants from being hunted, collected or sold.

▲ The European bison was once almost extinct. A few lived on in zoos. Now young bison, bred in zoos, live freely in a Polish national park.

▼ Wildlife reserves, like this one in Africa, are the last hope for some species. In the wild, they are in danger from over-hunting.

Glossary

Acid rain: this is rain that has been polluted by gases from factories, power stations and cars. These gases turn the rain into acid which causes many water plants and animals to die and trees to lose their leaves.

Atmosphere: the area that fills the sky and surrounds the Earth is the atmosphere. It is made up of invisible gases, such as oxygen and carbon dioxide.

Cancer: the growth of bad cells anywhere in the body. These bad cells destroy healthy ones and can spread all over the body. Doctors are now finding cures for some cancers using different kinds of plants.

Carbon dioxide: a gas that is colourless and invisible. It has no taste or smell. Plants would not be able to breathe without it.

CFCs: these are substances that are man-made and which destroy the ozone layer (a layer of gas in the Earth's upper atmosphere that stops harmful rays from the Sun coming down to Earth). These substances keep our refrigerators cool and are sometimes found in spray cans.

Chemicals: this is a word used to describe substances, each with their own particular features. They can be gases, liquids or solids. Oxygen and hydrogen are both chemicals and they can react together to form another chemical, water.

Cones: these are fruit that come from trees such as pines and firs. The cones carry seeds. If you shake an open cone lots of little seeds will drop out.

Crops: this is a word used to describe the growth and produce of a certain plant. If you have an apple tree, the apples that grow and drop to the ground are the crop.

Dumped: when you get rid of something, like rubbish, or tip it out, you have dumped it.

Ecology: the study of plants and animals and the particular place they live in.

Environment: the part of the air, water or land that an animal lives in is its environment.

Erosion: this word is used to describe the way land is worn away by the wind and water. For example, cliffs are worn down by both the wind and the sea.

Extinct: when all the animals of the same kind have died out, that kind is extinct. For example, the last passenger pigeon died out in 1914.

Fertilizers: these are substances that are put on the land by farmers to make the ground better for growing plants and crops. Sometimes they only help for a short time and then they make the ground poisonous.

Filters: specially made devices, used to clean the air by taking out dirt and harmful chemicals.

Fossil fuels: this is a term used to cover those sources of energy that have been made under the Earth's surface for millions of years. For example coal, oil and certain gases.

Grazing: when animals eat grass, they are grazing. When land is good for grazing, it means that it has enough grass for animals to eat.

Lead-free petrol: an engine runs on petrol that is a form of oil. As the engine runs, this petrol is used up and the parts of it that cannot be used in the engine are sent out through the exhaust pipe of the car. If the petrol is not lead-free, lead is sent out, which is poisonous. If petrol is lead-free it is safer for people, other animals, and plants.

Marginal: land that is mainly dry, but is not dry enough to be called a desert. Crops cannot grow on this kind of land, unless more water can be supplied.

Medicines: any substances that are taken by swallowing or by an injection that are used to treat illnesses and disease.

Methanol: a substance made from carbon, hydrogen and oxygen. It is a colourless liquid that is poisonous. It is found naturally in trees, but can now be man-made.

Micro-organisms: tiny living objects that can only be seen through a powerful microscope. Bacteria are micro-organisms.

Microscope: an instrument used to make very small objects look bigger.

Pesticides: any substance that kills pests. Pests are living plants or animals that do harm to other plants or animals.

Pollution: the act of spoiling or poisoning any part of the world around us. Pollution can be caused by exhaust fumes, dumping rubbish or chemical waste from power stations.

Rays: beams of light that come from a source, such as the Sun or a light bulb.

Solar system: this is a word used to describe the Sun, the plants that go round it and other objects like asteroids, meteors and comets.

Starvation: having nothing to eat or drink. If you are starving, you are slowly dying because you have nothing to eat or drink.

Sub-tropical: this word describes those areas that are close to the tropics (see **Tropical** below).

Tanker: a very large ship built to carry large amounts of oil, or other loads.

Terraces: steps cut into the hillside to stop the land from slipping away. People sometimes build these so that they can grow crops on them.

Transpiration: plants lose water through their leaves, having taken water in through their roots. This is called transpiration.

Tropical: a word used to describe very hot and wet areas of the Earth.

Vapour: This is a gas that has come from some substances that are normally either a liquid or a solid. When water is heated it turns into water vapour.

Windbreaks: these are structures that stop the wind from shifting the soil. For example, trees with their roots help to stop the earth from being carried away.

Zone: this is a word used to describe a particular area or region.

Index

A number in bold shows that the entry is illustrated on that page. The same page often has writing about the entry too.